Test your

Business
Skills

Test your

Business

Skills

**GENE CROZIER
AND GARETH LEWIS**

Series editors: GARETH LEWIS & GENE CROZIER

Hodder & Stoughton

A MEMBER OF THE HODDER HEADLINE GROUP

Orders: please contact Bookpoint Ltd, 130 Milton Park, Abingdon, Oxon OX14
4SB.
Telephone: (44) 01235 400414, Fax: (44) 01235 400454. Lines are open from 9.00
– 6.00, Monday to Saturday, with a 24 hour message answering service.
Email address: orders@bookpoint.co.uk

British Library Cataloguing in Publication Data
A catalogue record for this title is available from The British Library

ISBN 0 340 802421

First published   2001
Impression number 10 9 8 7 6 5 4 3 2 1
Year   2004 2003 2002 2001

Typeset by Fakenham Photosetting Limited, Fakenham, Norfolk.
Printed in Great Britain for Hodder & Stoughton Education, a division of
Hodder Headline Plc, 338 Euston Road, London NW1 3BH by Cox & Wyman
Ltd, Reading, Berkshire.

in *the Institute of Management*

The Institute of Management (IM) is the leading organisation for professional management. Its purpose is to promote the art and science of management in every sector and at every level, through research, education, training and development, and representation of members' views on management issues.

This series is commissioned by IM Enterprises Limited, a subsidiary of the Institute of Management, providing commercial services.

Management House,
Cottingham Road,
Corby,
Northants NN17 1TT
Tel: 01536 204222;
Fax: 01536 201651
Website: http://www.inst-mgt.org.uk

Registered in England no 3834492
Registered office: 2 Savoy Court, Strand,
London WC2R 0EZ

Contents

Introduction

The 'Test Yourself' series covers a wide range of skills, competencies, capabilities and styles that all contribute to our uniqueness as individuals and our performance in the workplace. Some of these qualities can be measured by objective tests that we call psychometric tests, but others are rather more complex and need to be assessed or evaluated using a range of other methods. Our ability to achieve business results is influenced by a complex pattern of behaviours, values and attitudes, whose impact on our employment success is described as 'personal effectiveness'. Not so long ago, the business leaders of the future were developed though the teaching of largely technical skills. Increasingly, organisations are looking for people whose repertoire of personal and practical business skills allows them to maximise their impact within and outside the organisation.

This book is half of a pair, and deals with the business skills that contribute to our success. The other book in this pair, *Test Your Personal Skills*, deals with some of the root causes of our business flair – our personal qualities and skills. Together they represent the two complementary facets of our personality that contribute greatly to success in life.

The chapters in this book follow the following sequence:

- **Chapter 1: The foundations of business success** – the background to the subject.
- **Chapters 2 to 7: Test your business skills** – an opportunity to assess yourself against a detailed inventory of business skills.

- **Chapter 8: More issues that affect business success**.
- **Chapter 9: Putting all the pieces together** – how to improve your skills.

By the end of the book, you should have gained a detailed insight into the key skills which contribute to your success, and identified some action points for the future.

The foundations of business success

Introduction

The search for the ingredients of personal and organisational success is probably as old as humanity. Certainly, from Greek and Roman times many great writers have been preoccupied by the question of what makes a successful leader. The diversity and success of books dealing with business success, with titles like *How to be Successful in Business, ... Make Your First Million, How to Become Your Own Boss*, prove the importance of the subject. Most of us want to achieve success in some form, yet finding a formula that we can use is not so easy.

In business terms, the models we use to identify and to develop business leaders have undergone considerable evolution over the last 150 years, so much so that managers are now confronted with an increasingly diverse set of philosophies, frameworks and tools to develop themselves and their employees. This diversity comes from the fact that there are radically different approaches towards the achievement of business success, each of which has its own merits and limitations.

The birth of personality theory
In the last century the seeds of modern personality theory in psychology were sown with the work of Galton. Galton examined the adjectives we associate with leadership, and from this huge lexicon of words started to cluster qualities under some main headings. This was to form the foundation of work by psychologists on the personality factors that influence an individual's behaviour.

Personality theory has now generated a considerable body of knowledge and tools in the form of psychometric instruments that are used increasingly by organisations to select and recruit their employees, owing to one simple fact – job performance can be predicted by an accurate assessment of personality and aptitude.

The age of scientific management
The twentieth century also saw the birth of modern scientific management, which was based on the notion that effective management lay in the knowledge of special techniques. This approach was supported by the emergence of mass production and in the importance of logistics during the two World Wars. The idea that successful management was all about theory and the application of special techniques led to the creation of a professional and an educational approach towards developing managers that is still reflected in the content of many management courses.

The competence-based movement
However, modern trends towards increased competitiveness and globalisation have forced many organisations to explore alternative approaches. In the UK, for example, the competence-based movement has revolutionised the whole approach towards management development, leading to the emergence of a whole range of new programmes that rival the traditional MBA, but also encouraging the transformation of many traditional programmes into a more practical approach. The movement grew out of a feeling that the way we developed our managers was too theoretical. It can be summed up by the phrase, 'it's not what you know, it's what you achieve that is important'.

Competence-based programmes therefore place a lot of emphasis on demonstrable, practical skills developed in the workplace.

A new approach

Yet even this practical approach does not provide all the answers. Faced with an increasingly complex and chaotic world, many companies are finding that the logical, functional approach to achieving results does not solve their problems or even necessarily improve performance. Today, we see an increasing number of successful companies, turning away from this functional approach towards a more inspired approach to identifying the recipe for individual and organisational success.

Here are several examples:

In a company specialising in tourist attractions and theme parks, the most highly valued skill of its employees is **customer care.** This is not the traditional view of customer care as a functional skill that can be taught easily, but rather as the special ability to make the customer feel good and really enjoy their day, even when weather conditions are not so good.

For a successful financial company based in the USA, the UK and Australia with many offices world-wide, the impact of several mergers taught them that, in their own words, it is 'the chemistry of the team' that matters the most. They talk about a focus on the feeling within the organisation – a sense of excitement, of appreciation of each other's qualities, of making the company a fun place to work. Individuals who can contribute to this 'chemistry' are special. They rarely recruit people through traditional means; instead, they 'court' potential employees through their networks. This approach also recognises the fact that individual success is also defined by, and dependent on, team culture.

The same approach is adopted by a technology company, which used to seek out professionally renowned individuals with good negotiating skills. Again they do not take a traditional view of negotiation, but focus on unusual individuals with the ability to think 'outside the box'. Most importantly, the people they recruit are able to see that the best technical solutions are not necessarily the best business or management solutions in the long term.

New approaches to management

It is obvious that there has been a significant shift in recent years away from the scientific approach to management towards a more sophisticated human relations approach. We have developed a deeper understanding of the fact that the motivation of workers is a key factor in their productivity at work. Organisations now have to work much harder to retain skilled staff and we now take it for granted that investment in people is as important as investment in other aspects of business or organisational life.

Organisational priorities are changing. This is the information age and the knowledge economy. We will surely see an acceleration of the growing importance of people's skills, capabilities and knowledge, and for many organisations it will be the most important or their only asset. Protecting intellectual capital in the form of acquired knowledge and people can only been achieved if you know what you have.

All of this explains the increased attention being paid by organisations to understanding the potential contribution individuals can make through a better understanding of what skills they can bring to the table, not just a matching of personality or technical skills to the nature of the business.

Increasingly, we see a greater dialogue between employers and employees in their joint search for success. Social contracts between the two are becoming increasingly sophisticated as organisations seek to combine strategic direction with performance management, employee incentive and reward schemes, and training and development within a single integrated framework. Individuals are increasingly able to place their personal aspirations and agendas high on the list of issues when talking to their employers.

The issues involved are complex, and people need a common language and models to move forward. This explains why the competency movement has found such favour in many organisations. Organisations are increasingly using the notion of competence to describe the skills that underwrite their organisational development. The particular blend of skills, knowledge, qualities and attitudes that go towards excellent performance at work are often explicitly called competencies, but are also referred to as personal effectiveness. Some of the most sought-after personal skills include:

- team working skills
- leadership qualities
- interpersonal skills
- customer care skills
- self-awareness and self development

A unified model

One very simple way of reconciling these different approaches is to view your actions as a process model. The *inputs* are who you are as a person, i.e. your *personal skills*, which in addition to inbuilt personal abilities, include your experience and expertise. You then apply these skills to the job in hand, and your ability to apply these effectively in a business context can be referred to as *business skills*. Finally, your success in this area can be measured by hard, quantifiable outcomes that are *functional skills* or *competences*.

As an example, let us take one important responsibility of a manager, that of *developing teams effectively*. It is obvious that this simple statement covers a wide range of skills, covering these three areas.

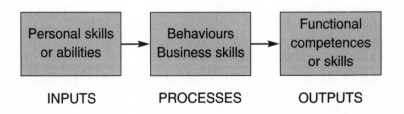

| Personal skills or abilities | Behaviours Business skills | Functional competences or skills |
| INPUTS | PROCESSES | OUTPUTS |

Personal skills
Some of the personal skills, which might make someone a great team-builder might include:

- **Empowering** – provides inspiration and motivates others.
- **Results driven** – wants to achieve results.
- **Development orientation** – believes in developing others – a natural teacher or coach.

These skills are a complex mixture of things – values, attitudes, personality factors, knowledge and experience. They are a melting pot of personal characteristics that define our preferences and capabilities. Most importantly, they represent skills *that can be applied to almost any situation*. The range of skills and qualities involved here are the subject of the sister text *'Test Your Personal Skills'* in this series.

Business skills
In every work situation, we can then turn these personal skills into a repertoire of roles, behaviours and actions that will have **impact** on the organisation and people around us. Our ability to transform personal potential into business results represents our business skills. For team development, these might include:

- **Managing change**
- **Negotiation skills**
- **Evaluating and improving business performance**
- **Team-building skills** . . . and so on.

The range of business skills that seem to be in demand from modern organisations form the content of this book. The different role models and management styles involved are also covered in *Test Your Leadership Skills* and *Test Your Management Style*.

Functional skills
Finally, our impact in a business environment can be measured through our ability to perform key tasks or achieve outcomes to a clearly defined standard. Many of these tasks will be more functional or technical in nature. In many ways, these types of skills (competences) are much easier to identify, because you can usually quantify some clear end product, e.g.

- Carry out effective appraisals
- Create effective development plans
- Generate effective proposals to gain support for the plans
- Coaching, counselling and mentoring skills
- Ability to train, run workshops etc.

The MCI Standards for Managers that form the base of many qualifications in management in the UK have been covered in the title *Test Your Management Skills* in this series. There are also a range of self-assessment aids in the series, dealing with specific functional areas, such as Finance or IT.

Of course, in real life we behave in a unified way and there is real overlap between these three approaches. However, this input-output model does match reality in that our business success is affected by the following:

- All three areas are closely interlinked and any weakness in one area will affect our total success.
- The ultimate source of our practical abilities lies in our repertoire of personal skills, which, whilst they may allow us to do almost anything, may be difficult to link directly to our achievements in the workplace.
- Many people tend to focus on visible outcomes rather than the underlying factors of success.

We hope this guide will encourage you to consider ways of developing your business skills in the future.

Summary

In this chapter, we have shown that the approach towards management development has followed the evolution of personality theory and industrial change. The main approaches towards measuring potential and success reflect an emphasis on:

- **The personal skills** or *competencies* of individuals that represent their potential to achieve results, based on complex personality factors, experience and expertise
- **The roles and business skills** people demonstrate within the total context of their working environment and
- **The functional skills** or *competences* that demonstrate an individual's ability to perform something in the workplace to a defined standard.

Each approach has its own advantages and disadvantages, but there is clear evidence that organisations are placing greater emphasis on the unique, individual skills of employees. Over the next five chapters, we will provide you with an opportunity to review your business skills in detail.

Test your business skills

Introduction

Now that we have described the background to the role of business skills in the workplace, we want to give you a chance to assess your own business skills inventory or profile.

The next five chapters cover the whole range of business skills. We have divided these into five families:

1. Focus on results
2. Commercial skills
3. Influence
4. Problem solving
5. Managing change

Each family represents a collection of individual skills or competences that fall under a natural grouping. Each chapter is structured in the following way:

A family overview, providing a general description, a map of the competences involved and guidance on good role models for this family of skills.
Individual competence definitions for each of the competences, containing an overview and examples of key indicators to help you judge your relative performance in this component.
The overall assessment section, allowing you to evaluate your performance in the family.
Developing skills, a section that provides specific advice on how to develop your skills in the family.

Family 1: Focus on results

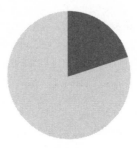

Business skills

As we apply ourselves and our talents within the world of work, one of the primary considerations is bound to be about success and achievement. Put bluntly, people in most working environments will judge us by the results we deliver. Also, for many of us, a key part of the personal satisfaction we derive from work is from the achievement of tangible results.

Some people are great thinkers, some are great organisers, some are great team players. But we reserve special accolades and rewards for those who can get things done. Thus it is one of the most highly valued families of skills at work.

It is related closely to the personal skills family 'getting things done'.

Overall, the family looks like this:

Focus on results

- Achievement focus
- Quality focus
- Time management

Illustration

'With a fixed gaze in mind, she will walk towards her goal. She can take in changes but nothing deters her.'

Talib Warsi on his wife, Perween, founder of S&A foods

As with all of the families, we shall ask you to think of people you know who might exemplify this family of competences. Before you examine each aspect of the family in more detail, try to take a more holistic view. Look at the map and try to think of people in your family or social life, in your work experience, or in the public domain, who you would judge to be excellent achievers or deliverers of results.

- What is it they have or that they do which makes them different from other people?
- What helps them to be so good at managing themselves?
- How much of this can I model or copy?

Achievement focus

This competence focuses on the ability to pay attention to

and deliver recognisable outcomes. People who score high on this competence tend to set high goals and achieve them. They focus on the completion of tasks, rather than immersion in a task for its own sake.

Illustration

'The best was for me to stop analysing and to start implementing. They were right because you can analyse something to death and get a perfect strategy only to find you're too late.'

Nick Reilly, chairman and MD of Vauxhall motors, on being asked the best advice anyone had given him.

What the illustration shows is that it is very important, not only to set goals and strategies, but to turn them into reality. The best thinking in the world is of little value if it is not acted on. This in turn implies that important aspects of this strand are:

- The ability to set goals and targets (to know where the goalposts are)
- To move from thinking to doing
- To stick with it despite setbacks

How can I spot high achievement focus?

Indicators
- Track record – achievements are usually publicly acknowledged
- Ambition
- Vision – can articulate future achievements
- Determination

- Taking control
- Favours action
- Sets high goals
- Decisiveness

Illustration

'Fortunately, there was someone in the lab who kept telling me I was a square peg in a round hole, and that spurred me on to prove myself. I have this bloody-minded perversity so if someone tells me I can't do something, I carry on doing it.'

Susan Greenfield, Professor of Pharmacology at Oxford University.

Quality focus

Although this family is very similar in terms of the underlying behaviours to the 'Getting things done' family in 'Test your personal skills', it is in the application of those skills in the business or organisational context that we are concerned with here. As the first strand concentrates on achievement per se, in this strand we look at the quality of the results. In the business environment, results are to do with the successful delivery of product, service and systems. What binds these together is that there are customers to be satisfied, and this is why quality of the outcome is important.

Illustration

'We were ecstatic when we won the French nationwide WLL licence in July. It was a very competitive situation and an extraordinarily attractive market, but the very next minute, we were back to thinking how to build it quickly. I am someone who would always ask the question, "If you had a great sales day, why wasn't it better?"'

Michael Price, co-founder of the internet venture Firstmark Holdings.

'There's no point in being spivvy and pushing something to someone one day if it's not the right product, because you will never get the chance to present to them again.'

Richard Davidson, co-founder of Brainspark, the internet incubator

Indicators
- Sets and communicates high standards
- Doesn't settle for second best
- Picks up on shortfalls in quality
- Conscientious
- Understands the needs of others – particularly customers
- Seeks to improve continually on output

Time management

Time management is really about being able to plan and organise our lives. In general, it is about being 'on top of things' rather than being submerged in the ebb and flow of the demands of everyday life.

Time management involves a number of things. Firstly, our activities should be goal-directed; that is, we are able to look to the future in terms of what we want to be doing and what we want to be achieving. This is in contrast to just 'taking life as it comes'. Then we are able to make choices in relation to our actions and efforts. We can prioritise, and we can make decisions about what is important as opposed to those things that are less important or relevant.

Finally, we are able to plan and organise our lives and our activities so that we work towards positive outcomes in an efficient manner.

We can recognise this in other people by:

Indicators
- Sets and works to objectives
- In control of events
- Pro-active
- Works to schedules
- Organised
- Aware of priorities
- Acts and works efficiently

Assessing focus on results

Test Yourself

Achievement focus

Low: Finds it difficult to articulate outcomes and goals. Takes too long to make decisions. Content to 'roll with the punches'. Lacking ambition.

Medium: Can deliver when pushed. Achieves completion on modest tasks, but not necessarily with the more major challenges.

High: Recognised as an achiever with a track record of results to show. A strong 'can do' streak. Shows determination in getting results and coming to successful conclusions. Knows the difference between winning and losing.

Role model	expert	competent	inconsistent	poor
⌃	⌃	⌃	⌃	⌃
1	2	3	4	5

self assessment ☐   third party assessment ☐

Quality focus

Low: Cuts corners and settles for second best. Unaware or unconcerned about standards. Sets a poor personal example. Doesn't learn from poor experience, and lacks continual improvement outlook

High: Sets high standards in output and methods of work. Sets a good example to others. Takes pride in quality of results. Intolerant of poor quality results.

Role model	expert	competent	inconsistent	poor
⌃	⌃	⌃	⌃	⌃
1	2	3	4	5

self assessment ☐   third party assessment ☐

Time management

Low: Always in a rush and seems to be 'behind' events. Reactive and fights fires. Disorganised. Does not plan ahead, or take control of priorities. Can work hard but not necessarily smart. Focuses on activity rather than results.

High: Works to clear objectives and goals. Plans work and activity schedules, and works to timetables. Organised. Focussed on results as opposed to activity for its own sake. Takes decisions on priorities. Gives the impression of being on top of events and in control.

Role model	expert	competent	inconsistent	poor
⋏	⋏	⋏	⋏	⋏
1	2	3	4	5

self assessment ☐   third-party assessment ☐

Average overall score for focus on results

self-assessment ☐   third-party assessment ☐

Developing your focus on results

List all of your achievements in the past few years. Compare these experiences with situations where you failed to achieve. What are the differences?

Check with colleagues, manager, family as to what they see as your achievements. Compare these with your own perceptions. What lessons can you draw?

List those things you want to achieve in the next month, year. Is this easy to do? If it isn't, you may need to focus more on results.

Review the proportion of your time spent productively working towards results. Is it enough?

Are you able to translate broad aims, goals, and even dreams into practical outcomes? Can you break a major task down into practical, achievable steps?

Look at the pattern of your own lack of achievements. Are these due to not being able to start on new projects? Or are they due to starting, but not being able to finish?

Family 2: Commercial skills

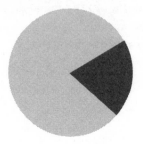

Business skills

We live in a very commercial and competitive world. Everybody these days has a customer. This is not just true for organisations, but for all the individuals within those organisations. Organisations in the public sector these days have to pay attention to commercial imperatives. Those who work in support functions are more than ever aware that, although the customers are internal, it is as important to address their needs as if they were end-user consumers.

Most of us, then, have to operate in a commercial environment, and to do so we need to be commercially aware, and we need to contribute to bottom-line benefits.

Not only this, but we have to be prepared to contribute to the commercial development and improvement of our organisations. Put together, these make a powerful set of forces that put innovation and entrepreneurial drive at the heart of the priorities of most organisations, and against which we will be judged.

This family encompasses the following:

- Understanding the broad business, commercial and economic environment
- Taking an entrepreneurial approach to the development of business ideas, and business development
- Understanding the commercial and business imperatives of your own organisation
- Being able to develop and drive ideas for improvement or innovation
- Managing the resources and processes to deliver bottom-line business results and outcomes

Illustration

'The other piece of good advice was from a financial controller in America who told me to "follow the roll of the coin". If you want to understand the business you have to understand the numbers because the numbers tell you why profitability goes down and the costs go up.'

Nick Reilly, chairman and MD of Vauxhall Motors

The family breaks down into the following competences:

Commercial skills
- Entrepreneurial skills
- Strategic perspective
- Managing resources
- Customer focused

Entrepreneurial Skills

'inclined to undertake and control an enterprise or business venture, especially one in which risk is involved'

Being able to do this involves a number of aspects. The first one involves commercial awareness. This is a complex mix of:

- Understanding the commercial environment and its realities
- The spotting of opportunities – this requires us to be future focused and imaginative
- Being able to evaluate viability of opportunities

The second aspect involves having business sense, which is an understanding of the context and environment of the particular businesses or markets in which you operate. This in turn involves:

- Understanding the key drivers of the business
- Understanding the commercial impact and consequences of decisions
- Keeping close to the commercial and competitive environment
- Interpreting key issues and framing them as decisions and actions
- Awareness of revenue and cost issues

The third aspect relates to the ability to manage risk. It includes:

- Awareness of actual and potential threats
- Being able to evaluate risk
- Taking controlled risks

Illustration

'... instead, I learned one of my first lessons in business, which was to listen and anticipate.'

Stanley Hollander, founder and chairman of Globalnet Financial

Strategic perspective

In any organisation it is important to have people who concentrate in their own field, or focus primarily on the affairs of their own function, department or business unit. Yet it is also important to understand how these fit as cogs into a bigger wheel. At every level in an organisation, there needs to be people who understand the picture at the next level, or the next few levels up. At or near the top of an organisation, it is vital to have people who also have a grasp of the whole context of an organisation, and then on to the competitive environment within the sector, and eventually within society and the economy as a whole. With our economies becoming increasingly global, the breadth and depth of knowledge and understanding needed can be formidable.

It is also important to be able not only to read situations but to project them into the future. Only if we can make reasoned and informed guesses at the shape of the future, can we hope to be prepared for it. This is what makes this competence area so important – especially in fast-changing service and technology based businesses.

Indicators

To be skilled in this area you need to be able to:

- Keep informed on wider political, social and economic issues
- Understand key aspects of technology and the opportunities it brings
- Keep informed on external environment
- Be able to view the 'big picture'
- Understand the drivers for organisational change
- Be able to assimilate and interpret complex information
- Be able to develop and communicate vision

Managing resources

As we gain seniority and management responsibility we gain charge of an ever wider range of resources. These resources for most managers, are wider than just cash. They include:

- Staff time and expertise
- Physical resources
- Knowledge
- Infrastructure
- Systems

To be a good manager of a portfolio of resources requires a number of skills. The first of these is being able to secure adequate resources for current and future needs. This involves being able to make a claim or a business case, which in turn involves analysis of resources required. It also involves an element of communication and particularly negotiation.

Next, we need to plan for the use of those resources. This involves understanding resource requirements and matching them to activities and outputs. It may involve the building of budgets, and other planning methods.

Finally, we need to monitor the use of those resources once they are deployed, and re-deploy pragmatically where appropriate.

Illustration

'. . .That the cash flow required to run a business doesn't bear any relationship to the profitability. You can have a business that makes £100,000 a year, but you may need a £1m bank overdraft to operate that.'

Tony Elliot, founder of Time Out magazine on being asked the first lesson he learned in business.

Indicators
- Make sound business cases and recommendations
- Negotiate to secure resources
- Analyse and evaluates options for use of resources
- Assess resource implications of options and decisions
- Plan for the use of resources
- Monitor the use of resources
- Construct a budget

- Aware of cost and resource issues
- Use resources efficiently and effectively
- Use resource management systems

Customer focused

As we emphasised in the overview to this family of competences, at bottom, all commercial organisations are about seeking out customers, and supplying products and services that satisfy their needs at a profit.

Organisations, in their missions, their culture, their operations and their training, continually have to reinforce the message that their success is based on satisfied customers. Therefore, the ability to understand and seek to meet the needs of customers is a vital competence area.

Illustration

'We always start with the user: We don't stand at the technical end and push it at the consumer. And so, thereby comes the task. The ethics of product design are bound up in this. There isn't an Excel spreadsheet on this one. It's not a science, but it contains science. It isn't an art, but it contains art.'

Richard Seymour, of designers Seymour Powell.

Indicators
- Knows who customers are – both internal and external

- Understands processes across the supply chain
- Understands needs of customers
- Responds to needs of customers
- Takes responsibility for customers needs and problems
- Committed to quality and improvement in product and service
- Deals with problems and complaints
- Develops relationships with customers
- Seeks feedback from customers
- Establishes systems for delivering and maintaining service quality
- Demonstrates leadership to staff in customer issues

Assessing your commercial skills

Test Yourself

Entrepreneurial skills

Low: Lacking in 'feel' for the commercial and competitive environment. Sees the world as it is rather than the opportunities available. Lacks appreciation of key drivers of business and revenue issues. Poor at managing risk.

High: Has 'radar' in relation to markets and external environment. Understands sources of revenue and value for the business. Is an opportunity spotter. Pursues ideas whilst evaluating and managing the risk.

Role model	expert	competent	inconsistent	poor
1	2	3	4	5

self assessment ☐   third party assessment ☐

Strategic perspective

Low: Uninformed or uninterested in wider issues and perspectives. Lacking in coherent views on the future. Naïve in terms of the way the commercial and business world works.

High: Highly realistic and informed view of the world. Able to see the bigger picture, spot patterns and trends. Future oriented, and able to articulate scenarios. Comfortable with complexity and ambiguity. Able to frame goals and objectives.

Role model	expert	competent	inconsistent	poor
1	2	3	4	5

self assessment ☐   third party assessment ☐

Managing resources

Low: Unable to convince others to support their plans. Often fails to take account of the full implications of their schemes and proposals. Finds it difficult to put together a full proposal or budget. Dislikes the hard skills needed for planning or budgeting. Poor project manager, often allowing tasks to slip and costs to mound.

High: Highly effecting at securing the resources required to achieve their plans. Creates convincing proposals and budgets. Keen awareness of the cost of activities. Enjoys keeping track of progress, brings projects back on track when necessary. Well equipped with a good range of financial and project management skills.

Role model	export	competent	inconsistent	poor
1	2	3	4	5

self assessment ☐   third party assessment ☐

Customer focused

Low: Poor knowledge and understanding of customers and their needs. Unresponsive to changing requirements. Poor appreciation of consequences of own actions for customers.

High: Knows who their customers are. Maintains contact and keeps informed of customer issues. Understands impact of own actions on customers. Goes the 'extra mile' when necessary.

Role model	expert	competent	inconsistent	poor
1	2	3	4	5

self assessment ☐   third party assessment ☐

Average/overall score for commercial skills

self assessment ☐   third party assessment ☐

Developing your commercial skills

Commercial skills have a great deal to do with knowledge and insight as well as experience. Perhaps unlike many of the other families in personal skills or business skills, this makes them very difficult to learn. None of them can be acquired through training or traditional book learning. Whilst this makes it difficult to develop our skills, it does not make it impossible. However, it does take time.

Two broad approaches are worth examining. The first involves knowledge and insight. A great part of this collection of skills is predicated on being informed about the commercial environment around you.

Key questions then become:

Do I know as much as I should about the key strategic issues and key drivers in my own unit or organisation?
Do I know the thoughts and perspectives of the main players?
Do I understand the needs of my customers and customer groups? What effort and methods do I use to get this information?
Do I understand what is going on in the market(s), and the wider business environment? What efforts and methods do I use to keep up to date?

If the answer to any or all of these is 'no' or 'not sure', then you need to look at some remedial action. Broadly, there are two main sources of knowledge. The first is published information. This can come from journals, newspapers, trade publications and the internet, among many others. If you don't know as much as you need to know, and if you are not up to date, you need to do something about it. In these days of the internet and intranet, there is little excuse.

The second aspect is what we might call 'intelligence'. This is the result of people using information to frame insights, perspectives and models of the world. The only real way to get this is through dialogue – talking to people. It is a networking issue. Do you come across the right people? And if you do, do you 'pick their brains' and find out what they are thinking, what they are doing, and what is coming around the corner?

The knowledge required in this family needs to be balanced by experience and your approach to work and to opportunities.

Do I think of my work in terms of the value to the customer? Do I pay attention to revenue, profit, new opportunities?
Am I willing to take a risk? Too willing?

Family 3: Influence

Business skills

What is influence? Influence is the ability to affect or change the behaviour or opinions of other people. It involves questions such as:

Do people listen to our position and ideas?
Why would anyone believe what I say?
Do they act on what we say?

In negotiations and discussions, can we set out a case and change the strategy or decisions of others?

It is easy to see why this range of skills is so important in business life. In leadership, in selling, in relating to customers, in representing our own interests or those of our department, we need to be able to change minds and influence opinions and decisions.

Influencing involves a number of underlying components. A basic foundation is clearly sound communication skills. Can we articulate ideas? Can we demonstrate understanding of key issues? Can we communicate a position, idea or decision? Related to this is the notion of being able to listen, understand and acknowledge the position of other people. It is difficult to influence other people if we can't communicate and convince them that we understand their interests and needs.

Other foundations for influence include:

The strength and attractiveness of our ideas, our strength of vision – do people know where we stand?

Credibility – do people have reason and evidence to believe what we say, and thus to respect our opinions?

Logic – our ability to persuade or convince by logical and rational argument, and the use of supporting evidence

Connectivity/networking – do we have strong relationships with opinion formers, the 'movers and shakers', or sources of political power?

Context – do we have and demonstrate an understanding of the basic issues and forces operating within our own context? Do we know what's going on in our own world?

Track record – have we 'been there and done that'?

These are all aspects that go to make up strong influence. To sum up:

The litmus tests for influence are:

- When we are consulted or asked our opinion
- When people believe what we are saying or are convinced by us
- When we are considered an expert or authority
- When we change the course of events

Influence
- Personal impact
- Building positive relationships
- Negotiation skills
- Networking
- Professional competence
- Integrity
- Communication
- Team skills

Personal impact

Sometimes called impression management. It involves consideration of how we come across to other people. We will have high and positive impact if we come across to people as professional, competent, thoughtful, organised, and if we have high standards.

Certainly, communication skills play a part here. But so do certain habits and styles of behaviour. These include:

Indicators
- Displaying confidence and conviction
- Showing an interest in people
- Being courteous
- Having energy or even dynamism
- Positive body language
- Good dress and appearance

Building positive relationships

There is a diverse set of skills which we apply to the business of initiating, building, maintaining and enhancing our relationships in life and work. It is in effect the bringing of our whole repertoire of personal abilities and applying them in relating to others in the working context.

As we have already pointed out, there is a huge range of types and levels of relationships that operate in life, and particularly in working life. Some are more formal than others. Some are nearer to friendships or even partnerships. Some are voluntary and are based on shared interest or 'spark'. Yet others exist because they have to (such as customer relationships).

In addition to the deeply human and personal aspect of relationships, there are some requirements that come purely from our professional relationship to each other. In these cases other issues come into play. These include:

Informing – telling people what they need to know and keeping them up to date.
Consulting – seeking opinion and input from those with a vested interest in what we do, or are about to do
Agreeing – achieving consensus or approval amongst interested parties to decisions, projects, initiatives and so on.
Checking – eliciting other perspectives. Checking understanding. Clarifying interpretations.
Respecting – the positions, needs of others, even if they are different to our own.

Anybody, whatever their personal style, can and does build

strong relationships. But some people have a higher level of sociability than others. If you are ease in the company of others, this is a great natural advantage. It is important to say that although sociability is influenced by our own introversion-extraversion tendencies, it does not mean that introverts cannot be sociable and cannot make strong personal relationships. But of course, relationships are about more than just being talkative. It is more a question of showing a willingness to spend time with others and taking an interest in their needs.

Negotiation skills

In the world of work, we rarely get our own way in everything. Business life is about balancing the interests of all the parties who have vested interests. Obviously, these interests can compete or even conflict. So, whether we are representing our own interests, those of our department or function, or those of the organisation itself, we need to be able to negotiate. Negotiation involves discussion and agreement to maximise the benefit to all interested parties. Notice that this is different to just getting your own way at the expense of the other party. In business life, we talk of 'win-win'.

People who are good negotiators can:

Indicators
- Represent the interests of own unit/organisation
- Understand and articulate own needs – 'must haves' and 'like to haves'
- Listen and respond to other parties

- Generate options and joint solutions that maximise mutual benefit
- Reach agreement

Networking

Networks are sources of power, knowledge and influence both within organisations and across organisations and sectors. Networking as a set of skills is co-dependent on a number of other families and competences dealt with in this book and in the companion *Test your personal skills*. Thus networking involves:

Indicators
- Being well connected
- Social skills, particularly in initiating, building and maintaining relationships
- Being willing to give as well as receive support and knowledge
- Investing time in relationships without immediate or tangible return
- Enjoying the company of others
- Being available and accessible
- Identifying the sources of knowledge and power and influence both within and external to your organisation
- Self confidence

Professional competence

One of the greatest sources of influence and credibility at a personal level is our own professional expertise. If we are 'an expert', or we have skills or knowledge that differentiates us from others, then we will be looked to for that knowledge and our opinions on relevant matters. We will be consulted as well as respected.

In all fields, knowledge moves fast, and we must work hard not only to keep up but also to stay ahead of the game.

Indicators
- Wide experience in our own field
- Source of knowledge and expertise
- Up to date with advances in own field
- Maintain professional development
- Take on challenges to enhance our knowledge, experience and expertise
- Able to market our skills and expertise

Illustration

'In *Creating Tomorrow's Organisations* (John Wiley & Sons, 1998), Susan Jackson and I predicted that "most organisations will only have a small core of full-time employees working from a conventional office. They will buy most of the skills they need on a contract basis, either from individuals working at home and linked to the company by computers and modems, or by hiring people on short-term contracts to do specific jobs or projects. In this way, companies will be able to maintain the flexibility that they need in order to cope with a rapidly changing world." '

Cary Cooper in People Management, Sept 2000.

Integrity

Integrity is about being authentic, or acting with good faith. It involves treating others with fairness and respect. It also involves keeping an ethical dimension and quality to our decisions, our actions, and in particular to the way we treat other people. Some of these things can be easily said, so the litmus test is if we can do this in difficult circumstances.

Indicators
- Saying what we mean
- Telling the truth
- Meaning what we say (being authentic)
- Distinguishing between right and wrong
- Respecting others – regardless of gender, race, class or culture
- Understanding the consequences of our actions and decisions – particularly for other people or groups of people
- Being fair in our dealings with others
- Not mistreating other people by lying, manipulating, bullying or otherwise abusing them
- Accepting the burden of our responsibilities

Illustration

'. . .to tell the truth because they always find out in the end . . .'

Tony Elliot, founder of Time Out magazine, on being asked about his business philosophy.

Communication

Communication is a theme that runs through many of the families of competence in this book as well as through *Test your personal skills*. In that book, we concentrated on the underlying skill of communicating primarily in one-to-one situations. In the working environment, there are particular aspects of communication that are expected and valued. These include :

Indicators

Written communication, which involves being able to:

- write in formats appropriate to the purpose and target audience
- write clear, simple and meaningful text
- use grammar and spelling correctly
- structure a document or report logically
- use word processor and e-mail fluently

Verbal communication (in one-to-one or group situations)

- articulate and express ideas clearly and with impact
- listen and respond to others
- gain rapport

Presenting information and ideas (to groups or audiences)

- structure a set of related ideas
- use voice tone and body language to gain and hold attention and interest

- speak with confidence
- deliver messages with impact
- use technology to aid presentation

Team skills

The importance of team skills in achieving business success is obvious, and there is significant overlap between the personal skills that support teamwork and the harder business skills involved in creating and developing successful teams. The hard skills involved include:

- Cultural awareness
- Team-building skills
- Coaching and facilitator skills
- Team-working skills

Indicators

Cultural awareness

- has a good understanding of the attitudes, views and feelings of individuals from different cultural or organisational backgrounds
- alters leadership and working styles to match the make-up of teams
- finds ways of resolving clashes due to differences in cultural backgrounds

Team-building skills

- enlists the help of all members of the team
- discusses issues openly and honestly
- removes any barriers to the success of a group
- uses a range of leadership styles and methods to get others to do things
- provides a real sense of vision and enthusiasm for the group's activities
- uses constructive feedback to build on the performance of the team

Coaching and facilitator skills

- regularly provides constructive feedback to others
- consistently identifies development opportunities for others and participates in their success
- finds ways of instilling enthusiasm and commitment for future plans and personal development
- sees learning and development as an investment not a cost

Team working skills

- able to balance the viewpoints and needs of others when working on plans
- uses a wide range of interpersonal skills to resolve conflict and encourage teamwork
- works well with others and is committed to the needs of the group

Assessing influence

? Test Yourself

Personal impact

Low: Low profile. Loath to push themselves forward. Hesitant or lacking in confidence in public situations.

High: Visible presence. Commands attention. Speaks with credibility and authority. Opinion former. Role models, have element of charisma.

Role model	expert	competent	inconsistent	poor
▲	▲	▲	▲	▲
1	2	3	4	5

self assessment ☐   third party assessment ☐

Building positive relationships

Low: Can tend to be a loner or 'stand-offish'. Employs habits of behaviour that disaffect people. Not widely trusted, included or sought out by others.

High: Generates warmth. Displays empathy and understanding of others. Invests time and interest in others. Has wide circle of positive relationships. Widely trusted.

Role model	expert	competent	inconsistent	poor
▲	▲	▲	▲	▲
1	2	3	4	5

self assessment ☐   third party assessment ☐

Negotiation skills

Low: Has difficulty in finding the balance between giving in and forcing own agenda in discussions. Poor skills in two-way discussions. Doesn't listen and respond to others.

High: Achieves results in discussions and negotiations. Able to represent their own interests. Generates win-win options and solutions.

Role model	expert	competent	inconsistent	poor
1	2	3	4	5

self assessment ☐   third party assessment ☐

Networking

Low: Poor relationship-building skills. Relationships are ephemeral or confined within small circle. Lacking in political 'nouse' or know-how.

High: Close to the sources of power and influence. Builds strong relationships across departmental, organisational and functional boundaries. Has wide circle of contacts. Available and accessible to others.

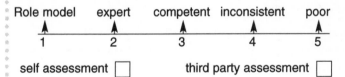

Role model	expert	competent	inconsistent	poor
1	2	3	4	5

self assessment ☐   third party assessment ☐

Professional competence

Low: Can seem behind the times in terms of knowledge. Invests little time or effort on own learning and development. Trades on past glories and achievements.

High: Acknowledged expert. Consulted by others. Keeps up to date and demonstrates leading-edge knowledge. Committed to learning and self-development.

Role model   expert   competent   inconsistent   poor
    ▲   ▲   ▲   ▲   ▲

1   2   3   4   5

self assessment ☐   third party assessment ☐

Integrity

Low: Inconsistent in behaviour. Doesn't command automatic trust of others. Doesn't always accept responsibility for decisions and actions.

High: Trusted and respected by others, and treats others with fairness and respect. Congruent behaviour – says what they mean, and does what they say. Will speak out against unacceptable or unfair behaviour. Makes decisions with integrity.

Role model   expert   competent   inconsistent   poor
    ▲   ▲   ▲   ▲   ▲

1   2   3   4   5

self assessment ☐   third party assessment ☐

Communication

Low: Has noticeable weaknesses in repertoire of communication skills and means. Not sufficiently paid attention to. Lacking in confidence in communicating one-to-one or to groups.

High: Communicates clear messages with conviction and impact. Has mastered a range of means of communication. Confident and fluent dealing with groups and in one-to-one conversation.

Role model   expert   competent   inconsistent   poor
    ▲   ▲   ▲   ▲   ▲

1   2   3   4   5

self assessment ☐   third party assessment ☐

Team skills

Low: Low level or negative contribution in team environment. Lacking in support of others. Uncomfortable or low profile in group situations.

High: Valued member of the team(s) they are involved in. Contributes substantially in team situations. Has identified strengths and roles in team context. Support others in the team.

Role model	expert	competent	inconsistent	poor
▲	▲	▲	▲	▲
1	2	3	4	5

self assessment ☐   third party assessment ☐

Average/overall score for Influencing

self assessment ☐   third party assessment ☐

Developing influencing skills

In this section we have treated the notion of influence as the combination of all of the communication and relationship building skills you need in the business context. This implies that there are two distinct, but not mutually exclusive ways of approaching the development of those skills.

The first of these is to take the idea of influence holistically. If you look at the notion of influence in itself, there are many things you can do, not only to increase your skills in the area, but to examine and improve your influence. This leads to two complementary considerations:

Influence who? Do you have relationships with the right people? Do you seek out yourself the sources of power and influence within (and without) your own department and organisation?

Influence how? Have you developed, and do you use the appropriate skills to put across the messages you need? Is it possible that you have the skills, but don't use them, or at least not in the right contexts or with the right people?

The second approach involves looking at the notion in a more atomistic way. That is, look at each of the competences that make up this family, and your scores for each. Where, within the family, are your strengths and weaknesses?

By examining your competence in these ways, you will quickly get a clear ideas of your potential areas for development.

Family 4: Problem solving

Business skills

This family of competences involves the use of reasoning and analytical skills applied to tackling real problems and issues. It therefore balances the cognitive with the very pragmatic. We can summarise this:

> Underlying ability + behavioural qualities + learnt skill = competence

Thinking skills are highly prized and rewarded in most organisations for good reasons. A look around at the modern economy and world of work will give some immediate clues. It wasn't that long ago when, for most adults, the primary skills were physical, as the world of work was based on manufacture and making things. We are now in the information age and the rules have changed. In our current economy, knowledge is itself the commodity in a lot of organisations. In these circumstances, the key skills for dealing with knowledge and information are thinking and analytical skills.

In addition, as organisations themselves change, and staff become more empowered – being enabled and required to make their own decisions, and to change and adapt at rapid pace – the skills involved in processing information, solving problems and making decisions become ever more important.

At the same time, this does not mean that the world is only fit for MENSA members. It is true that organisations do pay attention to our underlying cognitive skills (fluid intelligence, which you can read about in *Test your aptitude and ability*). However, if this is the 'raw material' that we as individuals have to work with, it is equally important that we are able to apply those abilities to the learning of practical and work-focused skills. This is a game that we can all join in.

Overall, the sort of processes involved include:

- Gathering and selecting appropriate information
- Sorting out important from the less important issues – making sense of a complex world
- Taking an ordered and structured approach to dealing with problems and decisions
- Generating creative options and solutions
- Evaluating options
- Making decisions – even in uncertain circumstances
- Evaluating impact and consequences of decisions

This family of competences involves:

Problem solving
- Analytical skills
- Systems thinking
- Creativity
- Decision making

Analytical skills

The foundation for these skills is our underlying cognitive ability. We possess a basic capacity to process various kinds of data. The ways we deal with data in itself involve a number of separate processes. These include: apprehending or capturing data by sense or intuition; making judgements about that data; and reasoning or the drawing of inferences, which then lead to knowledge or understanding.

There are very clearly strong individual differences in people's ability in terms of thinking skills. Whether these are by virtue of nature or nurture is a philosophical discussion for another place. However, we do seem to have 'natural' differences from person to person in our capabilities. Whatever the level of our natural capability, it needs practice and use for us to maximise the benefit. In the business environment, we also need to apply it pragmatically to the world around us.

Illustration

'There were many good things in the City ... my ideal was to take the best things – the brainpower, the intellect, the risk-awareness, the ability to get excited ... – and combine them with the best things in other industries.'

Stewart Dodd, co-founder of Brainspark, venture capital incubator

---

Indicators
- Able to process volumes of data

- Fluid ability to deal with verbal, numerical and/or abstract data and ideas
- Sets out reasoned, logical arguments
- Evaluates logical arguments and evidence
- Spots inconsistencies in arguments or conclusions
- Draws accurate conclusions from data
- Makes sound judgements

Systems thinking

Although the underlying skill here will be covered by the previous competence, this is more to do with how you apply those skills to the real and complex business environment on a large scale. The notion has been popularised by Peter Senge and his colleagues at Harvard, because they have identified it as a key set of skills (the 'Fifth Discipline'). It is seen as the ability to identify and understand the deep structure of dynamic forces that operate in the make up of dynamic systems. Systems are complex structures of interacting components such as biological systems, natural systems, and so on.

But economies, markets, human systems like organisations, and supply chains are also dynamic systems. They therefore have all the complexity inherent in those systems. What characterises such systems is:

- Ambiguity
- Complexity
- Conflict

Linear cause and effect chains are difficult to determine in such systems. Nonetheless, it is possible to identify patterns and trends, and more importantly, it is possible to model the behaviour of such systems. But it is a high-level skill.

Indicators

People who are good systems thinkers:

- Assimilate large amounts of data and information
- Identify deep underlying patterns
- Generate theories, explanations and hypotheses about that data
- Apply interpretation to an understanding of the way the world works
- Cope with complexity and ambiguity
- Take a broad system view of things
- Identify relationships between parts of a system
- Model complex situations

Creativity

Most of us admire creativity in people when we come across it in any walk of life. Creative thinking provides the 'spark' or the special insight that leads to innovation or developments in every aspect of human activity. Think of things that you admire in areas that interest you:

- Science
- The arts
- Politics
- Sport and human performance
- The media

We can think of specific innovations that involved someone, somewhere thinking in a different way, or somehow breaking boundaries. It is this unusualness, or uniqueness that so often characterises creative thinking. We call it 'thinking out of the box', which indicates that it is so often not obvious, and not derived by purely linear logical thinking. So not only do we admire the people who can contribute to such developments, but they are vitally important in moving along human culture and achievement.

Of course, in the business environment, creativity is also important in helping to harness technology to products and services, and to aid competitiveness.

There is a certain kind of creativity (with a big 'C') that is the territory of the genius. These are the Mozarts, the Leonardos, and the Einsteins. Very few of us can aspire to that kind of creativity. However, there is a different kind of creativity (with a little 'c'), which we can all access. In our own worlds, we can contribute novel ideas, insights, suggestions for improvements, solutions to problems, and so on. This kind of creativity still involves some or all of the following:

Illustration

'I believe in celebrating my team's creativity and their achievements more than my own. I came up with the My Bright Idea initiative, where staff can submit their ideas.'

Perween Warsi, co-founder of S&A Foods.

Indicators
- Having deep knowledge of our own subject or area

- Being able to view things from unusual perspectives
- Coming up with novel ideas or approaches
- Ability to 'ideate' (to generate ideas to order)
- Openness to new ideas and experiences
- Taking risks
- Not minding going against the flow
- Challenging ideas and assumptions
- Daring to be different
- Seeing opportunities
- Contributing to the planning and implementation of new ideas
- Generating options
- Ability to challenge orthodoxy and the status quo

Decision making

You will have noticed that this family of competences has a real practical bias. However good our underlying cognitive skills, in business we are measured by what we do with our thinking skills. This means not only dealing with problems and challenges in a purely analytical way, but ultimately in committing to decisions and actions. This competence, then, is about the process of moving from thought through decision towards action.

This has a number of aspects :

- the willingness and ability to tackle real problems and challenges
- the ability to make decisions – that is to be decisive
- the soundness of the decisions and the judgement demonstrated

Indicators
- Faces up to problems and challenges
- Seeks out appropriate information
- Consults others
- Takes an ordered and structured approach to dealing with situations
- Generates practical options and solutions
- Evaluates options
- Evaluates impact and consequences of decisions
- Makes sound judgements and decisions

Assessing your problem-solving skills

Test Yourself

Analytical skills

It is quite possible that you have a good idea of your own level of skill from various sources. Your level of educational attainment will give some clues. You may also have undergone psychometric testing which is aimed at giving an objective assessment of underlying analytic skill. Basic aptitude tests you may have done can give information on:

- general underlying fluid intelligence
- specific abilities such as verbal, numerical or abstract reasoning
- critical thinking and reasoning abilities
- ability in specific applied areas

Low: Finds technical or difficult problems hard to solve or frustrating. Avoids tasks that require detailed analysis. Performs less well on some aptitude tests.

High: Enjoys detailed analysis. Good grasp of the detail. Enjoys figures and difficult problems.

Role model	expert	competent	inconsistent	poor
1	2	3	4	5

self assessment ☐   third party assessment ☐

Systems thinking

Low: Lacking in perspective or the 'big picture'. Poor grasp of cause and effect. Uncomfortable with complex or ambiguous situations.

High: Can model or describe key features of systems. Has a grasp of relationships and patterns. Understands the dynamics of complex situations and systems.

Role model	expert	competent	inconsistent	poor
1	2	3	4	5

self assessment ☐   third party assessment ☐

Creativity

Low: Responds in predictable ways to challenges. Has difficulty with new ideas. Reluctance to think radically.

High: Always has new ideas or approaches. Able to 'think out of the box'. Challenges assumptions.

Role model	expert	competent	inconsistent	poor
1	2	3	4	5

self assessment ☐   third party assessment ☐

Decision making

Low: Reluctance to face up to challenges and problems. Poor or haphazard approach to dealing with problems. Indecisive. Makes rash or poor decisions.

High: Willing to face up to and tackle problems. Approaches problems thoroughly and systematically. Decisive. Makes good decisions using sound judgement.

Role model	expert	competent	inconsistent	poor
1	2	3	4	5

self assessment ☐   third party assessment ☐

Average/overall score for problem solving

self assessment ☐   third party assessment ☐

Developing your problem-solving skills

The first thing to do, if you have not already done so, is to evaluate your aptitude and ability. The indicators and the assessment section above should help you to do that. Whatever your level and scope of your abilities, you should never interpret them as meaning 'can't'. What they may help you to realise is why you perhaps feel uncomfortable or overwhelmed when faced with complex and ambiguous information.

A key theme in this family, is practical application. What is important therefore, is to apply the talents you have to the environment in which you work. Much of this is to do with doing your homework. Do you 'read up' on important issues? Are you aware of what is going on around you? Have you identified, and do you use good sources of information? Among the most important sources of information are the opinions of people who themselves are in the know, and people whose opinions you trust.

Once you begin to get more up to date with what is going on in your own organisation and its external environment, you need to look at what you can do with this information. People who are seen as poor problem solvers are those who bury their heads in the sand, and don't tackle situations as they arise. It may be you need be a bit braver in taking on the challenges that face you.

Good problem solving and decision making is all about applying a systematic approach – gathering good information, diagnosing problems, generating viable options, and so on. Good judgement comes with practice and experience. However, the better the information you gather, the better your decisions are likely to be. Trust yourself to be a little braver and more creative about the possibilities you consider. Learn to make the best possible use of the opinions and judgements of those around you.

Finally, there comes a time when decisions have to made, and action taken. If you feel you are indecisive or reluctant to take decisions at all, consider your own personal barriers to quicker or more forthright decision making. Review some of the decisions you have made in the past. This includes major life decisions like buying houses and cars, for instance. What are the circumstances in which you made the best judgements? And what about the worst? What can you learn from these experiences?

Family 5: Managing change

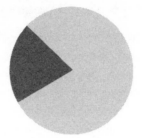

Business skills

The case for needing to be able to cope with and indeed manage change in the organisational context is overwhelming. It seems to be a component of the core competence of all organisations. Following on from this, we are required to embrace change, to manage it, and at the very minimum to be able to cope with it. Change in organisations comes in many and varied forms:

- New products and services
- New systems
- New ownership
- New organisational structures
- New technology and systems
- New relationships with customers and suppliers, partnerships
- Changes in culture and working practices
- New skills

Aside from these, there is the human side of this, which is that we are required to cope with the psychological and attitude aspect of these changes.

So there are some very work-related skills required to manage and thrive in circumstances where the changes in our list above are happening all the time.

We also have to manage our own mindset – our stress, outlook, ability to cope, to deal with the tensions involved, and so on.

Illustration

'Lots of things have happened to me by chance, but I do think you have to make the most out of opportunities when they arise and see them as a challenge. It's important not to be frightened to stick your neck out, and to recognise that when you do, people may not like you for it. You have to be brave.'

Susan Greenfield, Professor of Pharmacology at Oxford University.

This family of competences includes:

Managing change
- Vision
- Multi-tasking
- Project management

Vision

One of the key competences relating to our ability to manage change is to do with having a clear picture of where we want to go. This is just as true if we are to cope with changes that occur around us as it is to do with change that we initiate. This competence is therefore future oriented. Are we able to develop and articulate positive future scenarios? Can we convince other people, and thereby hope to carry them along with us?

Equally, are we able to let go of the past? Some people are poor at dealing with change because they are overly rooted in the past or in the status quo. Letting go is very important, but much more easily said than done. A key part of letting go is feeling comfortable with a personalised version of the future. This is what visioning is about.

Indicators
- Positive outlook
- Envisioning future scenarios
- Communicating and gaining commitment from others
- Able to let go
- Adaptable to changing circumstances

Multi-tasking

Working life is busy and pressured. The pressures of a competitive environment, together with organisational changes such as downsizing, de-layering, mergers and acquisitions, mean we all have more to do than there is reasonable time to do. Most of us have substantial portfolios of responsibilities, and we need to be able to switch from task to task, responsibility to responsibility, role to role and priority to priority.

Multi-tasking then, is about the ability to manage complexity in the work environment. It is also about the ability to lead a complicated life with many, sometimes competing, priorities and areas of focus.

Indicators
- Deals fluently with competing priorities
- Skilled in a range of roles
- Switches tasks and responsibilities easily
- Comfortable in changing circumstances

Project management

Managing change involves more than just having the right attitude. It requires skills to plan activities to achieve desired results. Much activity in business is based around projects. In fact, we can say that much change is delivered via major projects and initiatives. Such projects can range from the re-design of business processes and systems, through the development of new products, to major infrastructure developments.

Projects are one-off initiatives that deliver planned and specified outcomes. Major projects need breaking down into the individual tasks that then need to be planned into a sequence that leads to the end result.

Project management involves the 'harder' skills that enable us to manage in a structured and organised way the tasks needed to achieve that result. There are a number of structured methods for managing major projects and initiatives. Whilst this is not the place to set out those methodologies, what is reassuring is that project management as a repertoire of skills is **learnable**.

Indicators

- Anticipate and secure required resources
- Use planning tools
- Build schedules of work and activity
- Consult and communicate with staff
- Monitor progression
- Keep to timetable and budget
- Drive progress
- Seek completion of tasks

Assessing your change-management skills

? ## Test Yourself

Vision

Low: Rooted in status quo. Overly pessimistic or fearful in their outlook. Unable to articulate clear vision.

High: Builds future scenarios. Able to articulate and communicate vision. Positive frame of mind.

Role model	expert	competent	inconsistent	poor
1	2	3	4	5

self assessment ☐   third party assessment ☐

Multi-tasking

Low: Low tolerance for changes in pace, task and role. Copes poorly with changes in direction. Able to focus on only one task at a time.

High: On top of events – even in turbulent times. Able to switch roles and tasks seamlessly. Can 'juggle without dropping the balls.' Copes with switches in direction and priority.

Role model	expert	competent	inconsistent	poor
⬆	⬆	⬆	⬆	⬆
1	2	3	4	5

self assessment ☐   third party assessment ☐

Project management

Low: Poorly organised. Lack of task planning. Fails to anticipate resources required. Assumes projects will manage themselves. Fails to involve or inform people appropriately. Poor record of project completion.

High: Uses planning tools appropriately. Works to project plan. Involves others in planning and delivering projects. Anticipates requirements and manages resources. Completes tasks.

Role model	expert	competent	inconsistent	poor
⬆	⬆	⬆	⬆	⬆
1	2	3	4	5

self assessment ☐   third party assessment ☐

Average/overall score for managing change

self assessment ☐   third party assessment ☐

Developing your change management skills

Developing skills in this area is easier said than done. One reason for this is that it involves a change of mindset. We have to learn to cope with uncertainty and anxiety, and our response in these circumstances might be quite deep seated. The first aspect of this is to try to develop a more positive outlook to changes that occur, or that might occur. Can you think of changes in your life or personal circumstances where you 'came through', despite anxiety and uncertainty? It is good practice to reflect on some of the major changes that have taken place in your own experience. This is particularly true of major changes related to work. Changes of job, changes of organisation or ownership, promotions, and so on.

- What helped you personally to cope?
- What were the barriers to you embracing the change?
- How quickly did you adapt?

If you make good guesses about what might happen in the future, and then strategise around that, you will be better prepared. What is the worst that can happen? What would I do then?

Looking at the skills themselves, we should all be able to develop a more robust approach to these planning and coping skills. Project management is about becoming more ordered, more organised, and more systematic in our approach to changes. In short, it is about being proactive and future oriented rather than reactive and rooted in the present. A common thread in all the change-management skills is planning and preparing yourself for the future, and managing your time in order to meet the challenges.

More issues that affect business success
Introduction

So far, our logical approach may have given you the impression that business success can be predicted simply by rating yourself according a list of relevant skills.

Unfortunately, life is not that simple. Each of these business skills is a complex, multifaceted and changeable set of behaviours. Often they cannot be treated in isolation, but rather as part of a total package you offer to the outside world. In addition, their impact is profoundly influenced by the context in which you operate. We would like to turn now to consider four of the factors that will profoundly affect your business success, namely:

- Personality type
- Role models
- Motivational factors
- Cultural differences

Personality type

Successful people are rarely ordinary, even if they do claim otherwise or yearn sometimes to join the rest of the crowd. It is often the extremes in our personality make-up that make us stand out from the rest of the crowd. These extremes can be seen as strengths or weaknesses (one wise saying says that our weaknesses are simply overplayed strengths), depending on your viewpoint. More to the point, the selection of senior executives often places a high emphasis on how unusual applicants are on scales that measure their social boldness, drive, ambition and independence.

The business skills reviewed in the last five chapters are themselves highly dependent on personality type. In many ways, the behaviours you display in the workplace can be viewed as the end product of a complex chain of internal processes, that start with your innate abilities and preferences but which are then are translated into the conscious thought processes that form the basis of your actions by acquired attitudes, knowledge and experience.

Individual elements of behaviour	collections/patterns of behaviour
Individual elements of behaviour	collections/patterns of behaviour
Individual elements of behaviour	collections/patterns of behaviour

Many key business skills are profoundly influenced by personality. This is either because you will find some things much easier to do, because of your personality, or because your personality will affect the way your behaviour appears to the outside world. If you are a natural extravert and socially bold, for example, you will find it much easier to enjoy and perform at formal social occasions than someone who is a natural introvert.

?

Test Yourself Exercise: The Big Five

Most multiple factor personality questionnaires identify five major dimensions or aspects of personality. Review the table below and try to position yourself on each of the five dimensions, using the descriptions at either end of the scale.

More issues that affect business success

	Strongly Agree	Agree	Unsure	Agree	Strongly Agree	
INTROVERT Quiet, reserved. Happy to work on their own. Don't actively seek out others. Often uncomfortable in social situations. Like solitary activities. Can be seen as shy, aloof, solitary. Don't need moral support.						**EXTRAVERT** Happiest surrounded by others. Like social interaction. Socially confident. Like working in groups, collaborative. Often assertive and bold.
GROUP ORIENTATED People-orientated, empathic and sensitive. They are more concerned about the needs of others than getting the task done. Careful, cautious and accommodating they will be easily influenced by others and are easily hurt.						**INDEPENDENT** Alert, quick to respond, decisive and self-assured. Like change and being active. Often challenging, they rarely take 'no' for an answer and place more value on their own feelings than the views of others.
SENTIMENTAL Love ideas. Intellectual. Like new and innovative approaches to life. Like artistic things and generally creative						**TOUGH-MINDED** Realistic, practical and conservative in their attitudes. Abstract things, especially feelings, tend to feature little in their decisions. They prefer practical, tried-and-tested solutions. Like to do things. Unsentimental.
OPEN Like to experiment with open minds. Tolerant. Inclined to bend the rules, dislike routine or procedures. Creative. May like to take risks.						**CONFORMING** Conservative and conscious of rules. Like order in their life. Self-disciplined. Strong sense of right and wrong. Risk averse. Value integrity and tradition. May dislike change.
CONFIDENT Calm, composed and satisfied with life. Relaxed and assertive, comfortable with themselves. Optimistic and positive.						**ANXIOUS** Tend to worry about things, often tense. Easily affcted by circumstances and by what people say. Tend to look to the future. May be suspicious of others.

Your preferences on each of these scales will influence the ease with which you operate the repertoire of personal and business skills described in the last few chapters.

In your personal inventory, there will be highs and lows for your business skills. The table below identifies some of the typical matches between personality type and key business skills. Examine the table below and see if there is any match between your own evaluation of personality type and your agreed business skills inventory.

INTROVERT		Networking skills Communication	EXTRAVERT
GROUP ORIENTATED	Team skills Customer focused Relationships	Achievement focus	INDEPENDENT TOUGH-MINDED
SENTIMENTAL or	Strategic thinking Systems thinking Creativity	Quality focus Negotiation skills Decision making	CONCEPTUAL
OPEN	Entrepreneurial Multitasking Vision	Time management Managing resources Professionalism Integrity	CONFORMING
CONFIDENT		Analytical skills	ANXIOUS

Of course, this is a great over-simplification and does not mean, for example, that if you are an introvert you will be a poor networker or communicator. But what is true is that extraverts will probably get a good head start, because of their natural preference to be with people. Good managers do compensate for their personality preferences and learn to operate at the 'other end of the scale', a skill better known as *emotional intelligence*.

Role models

The business skills we have identified represent a form of inventory of skills that can be mixed and re-assembled to meet a variety of different jobs or to fulfil different behavioural roles. This is one of the reasons why people are often surprised to discover they do something well when the pieces are reassembled by chance.

We can use your own personal inventory produced in the last chapters to analyse the nature of successful performance in key areas, and to examine the degree of fit between the qualities required and our own personal inventory.

WORKED EXAMPLE

Let's look at the role of a consultant. Whether you are a management consultant or not doesn't really matter. At some time, we are all called in to provide advice and support to others, either internally or to our clients. We all have a mental image of a consultant, yet the role is surprisingly complex and contains a number of very different aspects. Here are just a few and we have chosen this example also to illustrate the power of images when dealing with roles.

• trouble-shooter	• coach	• specialist
• change agent	• facilitator	• researcher
• designer	• teacher	• auditor
• magician		• analyst

All of these roles require different sets of skills and qualities. The type of person who will make a good auditor is quite different from an effective trouble-shooter, which in turn will be quite different from someone who fits a facilitator role.

Review these models and identify which of these roles offer the 'best' and the 'worst' fits to the way you operate at work. Then ask yourself why this is so, by reviewing the business skills required to fit each role. By the time you have completed this task, you should have gained considerable insight into the critical skills from the overall inventory.

Motivational factors

The fundamental drives that cause us to behave in particular ways are referred to collectively as motivation. In traditional psychology, basic needs and wants drive us towards our goals and orientate us towards particular activities. According to Maslow, there is a hierarchy of needs starting with basic physiological needs such as food, water, a roof over our head, through social needs right through to our highest ambitions for achievement.

However, this theory is not really very helpful – it certainly doesn't inform us about why we are feeling the way we are, just at this moment. It doesn't explain sudden shifts in emotion and mood, or the reasons why people often seek danger or engage in self-destructive activities.

Professor Apter from Georgetown University in the States has offered the world a more practical model to explain all of this. In his Reversal Theory, he proposes that individuals shift constantly from one mode of thinking to another, and that it is often these shifts that bring about our most intense emotions.

His model proposes eight motivational states in four pairs, i.e.

SERIOUS focusing on goals, planning and avoiding surprises or anxiety.	PLAYFUL focused on enjoyment, acting spontaneously, creating excitement and taking risks.
CONFORMING, a state of mind orientated towards obligations and the maintenance of rules and routines.	CHALLENGING, a questioning, assumption-testing state of mind orientated towards personal freedom.SYMAPHY, driven by
MASTERY, which focuses on power, control and dominance.	security, caring and general harmony.
SELF-ORIENTATED and centred on one's own needs.	OTHERS-ORIENTATED, in which the needs of others figure most prominently.

Each of these states satisfies different emotional needs and we experience them not singly, but as combinations of one of each pair, although one or two of these will tend to be more dominant at any point in time. One key argument in the theory is that all eight states contribute to good mental health, and that a person needs to become skilful in meeting the needs of all eight states through his/her behaviour and activities.

By the way, if you have already noted some similarity between this framework and the Big Five personality factors discussed under personality type, you are quite right. Clearly these factors do have a role to play in the underlying factors that influence overall motivation.

Michael Apter's theory is more than just a nice piece of academic research, because it has been able to provide experts with practical tools to increase success in individuals, for example:

- Clinical psychologists and doctors have been able to deal with issues of drug abuse, deviant behaviour and mental illness by using the model to identify the source of supposedly damaging behaviour.
- Sports coaches have achieved amazing success in athletes by providing them with an emotionally rich environment that deals with issues of boredom and fatigue.
- Organisations are beginning to improve performance by providing a richer emotional environment and checking the correspondence between the supposed culture of the organisation, the key motivating factors for employees and the reality on the 'shop floor'.

So, what does all this mean in practice and how can you use this knowledge to manage your own career more effectively? Well, the main advice we can give is to recognise that the difficulties we experience in exploiting our business skills to the full come from all this complexity. We need to be realistic and become more aware of our own fluctuations in life, for example:

- Personal action plans are developed as logical and linear plans, but they rarely work out that way. Most people go through phases of intense development and progress, followed by periods of relative calm. Look at your personal history – do the peaks come at regular intervals, and are they generally during times of personal upheaval or when conditions are ideal?
- Motivation will go through cycles. Learn to deal with the

depression and the disappointments, and learn to turn them into constructive action.

- Ask yourself whether you are getting enough variety in life through your work. Your organisation may not match your own motivational style. Your business effectiveness will be improved significantly by ensuring that this is the case.

Cultural differences

There are very few organisations today that are not international in some sense. The global market is forcing most of us to interact with other cultures on a day-to-day basis. International experience is seen as increasingly important for the new generation of managers entering the world of work and is reflected in the content of management qualifications like the MBA. But it is also reflected in our appreciation of the different cultural perspectives on what makes for successful management.

In fact, many of the models and thinking that percolate into the business community through the latest trends or bestsellers on the book lists are themselves strongly culturally biased, in that most of them come from the USA with a strong Anglo-Saxon influence. Even our understanding of the role of a manager is culturally biased.

For example, examine the four descriptions of a manager below. Which one do you favour, and which does your organisation promote?

1. **The traditional view**, based on control, rational analysis and a dislike of uncertainty. Managers as **organisers** are there to steer the organisation through difficulties and to achieve results.

2. **The entrepreneurial view**, based on an experimental approach to life and ability to take on risks. Success is based on creating the future, not waiting for things to happen.
3. **The professional view**, based on technical knowledge and group norms. Success is based on the effectiveness of the organisation created through good **technical knowledge**, **planning** and management.
4. **The humanistic or facilitative approach**, in which the manager seeks to facilitate the work of the group and of individuals. Tasks matter less than the health of the group.

All of these models are legitimate and predominate in different regions of the world and in different organisations. Each has its own advantages and disadvantages. In the last section, we showed you how to build up a range of profiles to match different roles. In just the same way, the business skills you will need to be successful in any one of these models will be quite different from the others.

Even in functional areas of management, there are wide differences in approach. In quality management, there is a wide gulf between the Total Quality or *kaizen* approach, based on a more Eastern philosophy, and the hard, Business Process Re-engineering approach.

This point is really important when it comes to your business success. One key ingredient in the recipe for success is to make sure that the model that suits you also suits the organisation(s) you work for. This may seem obvious, but a mismatch is often the cause of problems for many managers. Faced with a feeling that things are not going as well as they would have liked, there is a natural tendency to say 'maybe I'm not so hot!', but in fact it is possible that there may be a cultural clash involved. There are countless examples of people, who have known spectacular success or disaster simply by changing organisations. Usually, the individuals are blamed or praised, but no-one really asks how much the organisational culture is the cause.

Of course, one alternative is to develop the roles and skills associated with different leadership models, and of course effective managers do indeed do that in developing their emotional intelligence. However, that all takes time and does not cancel out the fact that you are more likely to do well when you work with role models that suit your personality.

Summary

In this chapter, we have explored some of the more complex factors underlying the application of business skills and their contribution towards personal success. In particular, we have reviewed the following:

- The role of personality type in determining our repertoire of hard skills.
- The relationship between business skills and the more complex behavioural roles we fulfil.
- The importance of motivational factors in success.
- The role of culture in the fit between you, your organisation and your working environment.

In the next chapter we will review how to make the best of the business skills inventory that you assessed in Chapters 2 to 6.

Putting all the pieces together

Introduction

So far, we have covered quite a lot. Over the last seven chapters, you should have built up quite a comprehensive profile of your business skills. In the last chapter, we identified issues that complicated the linkage between this profile and success, but which could also offer more insight and control over this repertoire of skills.

In this chapter we shall provide you with general advice on how to apply this knowledge to further personal development.

Mastering your business skills inventory

The sheer volume of books on achieving success, along with the popularity of time-management courses and devices to give up smoking, illustrates one key fact – that people generally find it very difficult to change their behaviour. One difficulty people experience in altering behaviour is that it all sounds very easy, but is in practice much more difficult.

The success factors involved are actually the same as those required in changing bad habits, such as smoking or gambling. To change behaviour, you need to remember the following:

- It takes time and patience to achieve significant results.
- You need all the help you can get.
- You have to want to change and this must be linked to clear benefits.

- At the heart of your behaviour lie your basic beliefs and values. Once these change, everything else follows. Unlike practical skills, these values can be changed overnight, but this will only happen through insight or trauma.

You have probably already identified business skills that you would like to develop. Of course, we can all produce a long list of wishes like 'I wish I were more outgoing, assertive, creative, aware of the needs of others....', just like a New Year's resolution list, but unless we can turn these into action plans, driven by success, the chances are they will just disappear and be forgotten in time.

To convert knowledge of your own business skills into action and success, you need to do three things:

- Raise your level of self awareness, including the source of your motivation
- Identify your key development needs and the reasons why you want to change
- Create realistic action plans

Raising your awareness – know thyself

As every good sports coach knows, the key ingredient for improved performance is **raised awareness through constant feedback**. The same principle is used by the masters of martial arts or Zen to achieve almost superhuman feats of strength and skill.

In the workplace, this means we should pay attention to our overall performance on a regular basis (awareness) and overcome any reticence in seeking feedback. Frequent and regular feedback is the only way to increase your awareness of your business skills. Look for different sources – self assessment tools, your colleagues, your boss, your partner and friends, even customers. Find ways of asking them what they think.

As we discussed in the last chapter, identifying the things that really motivate us to perform well is also important. If we don't have a handle on these and use them to power our development, we are likely to achieve far less in our lives.

Identifying development needs and creating your vision

The self-assessment exercises will certainly have identified things we need to develop. But we also need to link these to the reasons why we seek change. One good place to start is to review your current job, previous career and the effect of your organisation and environment to gain more insight into your personality and what you want from life, e.g.

How well do you suit your current job? Which aspects delight you and which do you find frustrating? Are you moulding your career to suit your personal preferences and to develop them, or is your career changing you? How separate is your home and social life from the workplace? How different are you outside work? Do you have regrets, things you want to do still? Why?

What is your ideal job? What is the environment like? Who would be your colleagues? How would you work? Why?

These are dangerous questions to some people, usually because they feel anxious about the answers and don't want to 'take the lid off'. However, they are also liberating questions and critical to keeping your life in your hands. Only by identifying what you want out of life, can you begin to match these aspirations to your personality and to identify future action points. Senior managers are particularly prone to ignoring this aspect of their lives; after all, they have reached the top and can't really afford to change direction at this stage.

Creating a realistic action plan designed to ensure success

Assuming that you wish to develop your career, you should use any feedback or self-knowledge to identify priorities for development and an action plan for the future. This is, of course, the difficult part. Here are some general guidelines for developing your action plan.

- *Gauge your readiness for improvement* – just how ready are you to step out into the 'spotlight' and to address critical work performance issues?
- *Relate your development needs to your current job and career aspirations* – always check out your feelings and gut reactions to feedback or guidance (such as appraisals) carefully. You may not want to change. Unless your action plans link up with your core values and personal aspirations, you will find progress difficult.
- *Focus on clear, manageable goals* – build success into your plans. Don't take on too much at once, look for short-term objectives with clear benefits for your

career that fit longer-term goals and above all make your objectives SMART– **s**pecific, **m**easurable, **a**chievable, **r**ealistic and **t**ime-constrained.

- *Look for models of best practice* – model your future success on others. Look for people who embody the skills you admire, build in opportunities to watch them at work or even better to work with them, and talk to them about how they think and how they acquired their skills
- *Set up processes for on-going support and feedback* – as we discussed earlier, your plans need to offer ways of improving self awareness and feedback, for example:

- Going it alone is always more difficult. Build your own support network, perhaps with colleagues who meet to discuss common problems. Recruit others to help you practise new skills, such as your boss.
- Actively seek out feedback on your performance. Don't wait for formal evaluations. Make sure you get positive, constructive feedback. Negative, non-constructive feedback is to be avoided.
- Learn and master steps for increasing your awareness and self-control.
- Try to anticipate your 'hot-button' responses to situations where you do things inappropriately and try to prepare yourself to recognise these and take action. Find a colleague who will signal to you when you are doing something inappropriately

- **Expect setbacks and build in your own rewards** – if progress seems too hard or slow, consider the possibility that you may be expecting too much from yourself or the organisation. Be more realistic. Allow for setbacks. Success needs reward to sustain it. This simple fact is often overlooked. Find ways of rewarding yourself, even if it is only a special treat. Celebrate your successes.
- **Evaluate progress regularly** – review, review and review! Be realistic and be prepared to adjust your plans if necessary.

General comments on identifying development opportunities

Training programmes are an obvious way of developing your business skills, but there are many other ways in which you can develop your skills without having to take time away from work or spend money. In trying to design an action plan for your future development, try to consider a range of in-house solutions that will broaden your practical experience and raise your profile. These might include:

- Using a mentor or coach within the organisation to identify development opportunities.
- Employing a greater variety of assessment tools to evaluate your skills effectively. Ask HR specialists for help in this area.
- Job shadowing, sharing or exchange schemes. These can be an effective way of learning how others do their work effectively.

- Special secondments to organisations or units that are centres of excellence for the skills you wish to develop.
- Participation in company-wide special projects to develop key initiatives.
- Self-help or action learning groups.

Above all, remember that effective managers possess broad management skills and can operate in a wide variety of situations. Try to avoid just concentrating on development within your professional area of expertise.

And finally...

It's a fast moving world and organisations are becoming very creative about how to get the best out of their people. Keep abreast of these changes by reading round the subject and talking to people from other disciplines. They may be able to point you in the direction of some very simple but effective development tools.

Summary

Creating effective action plans to strengthen business skills and further success is not always easy. Long-term success will depend on your ability to:

- Raise your level of awareness
- Identify your key development needs
- Create realistic action plans
- Review your plans constantly and keep abreast of the latest developments

Good luck with your plans.

Useful addresses

The British Psychological Society (BPS), 48 Princess Road East, Leicester LE1 7DR Tel: 0116 254 9568. Fax: 0116 247 0787.

The Institute of Management (IM), Management House, Cottingham Road, Corby, Northants, NN17 1TT Tel: 01536 204222.

The Institute of Personnel and Development (IPD), IPD House, Camp Road, London SW19 4UX Tel: 020 8971 971 9000.

Test Suppliers and Publishers

Oxford Psychologists Press Ltd, Lambourne House, 311–321 Banbury Road, Oxford, OX2 7JH Tel: 01865 311353.

The Psychological Corporation, Foots Cray, High Street, Sidcup DA14 5HP

Psytech International Ltd, The Grange, Church Road, Pulloxhill, Beds, MK45 5HE Tel: 01525 720003.

Saville & Holdsworth Ltd, 3 AC Court, High Street, Thames Ditton, Surrey, KT7 0SR Tel: 020 8398 4170.

The Test Agency, Cray House, Woodlands Road, Henley on Thames, Oxon, RG9 4AE Tel: 01491 413413.

Further reading

Boyatzis, R. *The Competent Manager: A Model for Effective Performance*, John Wiley & Sons, 1982.

Chapter 9

Crozier, G. *Test Your Personality*, Hodder & Stoughton, 2000.

Crozier, G. & Lewis, G. *Test Your Personal Skills*, Hodder & Stoughton, 2001.

Goleman, D. *Emotional Intelligence*, Bantam Books, 1995.

O'Neill, B. *Test Your Leadership Skills*, Hodder & Stoughton, 2000.

Pearn, M. & Kandola, R. *Job Analysis – A Practical Guide for Managers*, IPM, 1988.

Senge, P. M. , Kleiner, A., Roberts, C. Ross, R. & Smith, B. *The Fifth Discipline Fieldbook*, Nicholas Brealey Publishing Ltd., London, 1994.

Smith, M. & Robertson, I. *Advances in Selection and Assessment*, John Wiley & Sons, 1993.